The Production
of Security

The Production
of Security

Gustave de Molinari

Translation by
J. Huston McCulloch

LvMI
MISES INSTITUTE

This essay was originally published as
"De la production de la sécurité," in *Journal des Economistes* (February 1849): 277–90.

This translation by was originally published as Gustave de Molinari, *The Production of Security*, trans. J. Huston McCulloch, *Occasional Papers Series #2* , Richard M. Ebeling, ed. (New York: The Center for Libertarian Studies, May 1977).

Ludwig von Mises Institute
518 West Magnolia Avenue
Auburn, Alabama 36832
www.mises.org

ISBN: 978-1-933550-57-2

The interests of the consumer
of any commodity whatsoever
should always prevail over
the interests of the producer.

— Gustave de Molinari

C O N T E N T S

Preface

By Murray N. Rothbard (1977)

Never has *laissez-faire* thought been as dominant as it was among French economists, beginning with J.B. Say in the early nineteenth century, down through Say's more advanced followers Charles Comte and Charles Dunoyer and to the early years of the twentieth century. For nearly a century, the *laissez-faire* economists controlled the professional economic society, the Societe d'Economie Politique and its journal, the *Journal des Economistes*, as well as numerous other journals and university posts. And yet, few of these economists were translated into English, and virtually none are known to English or American scholars—the sole exception being

Frédéric Bastiat, not the most profound of the group. The entire illustrious group remains unstudied and unsung.

The most "extreme" and consistent, as well as the longest-lived and most prolific of the French *laissez-faire* economists was the Belgian-born Gustave de Molinari (1819–1912), who edited the *Journal des Economistes* for several decades. The initial article of the young Molinari, here translated for the first time as "The Production of Security," was the first presentation anywhere in human history of what is now called "anarcho-capitalism" or "free market anarchism." Molinari did not use the terminology, and probably would have balked at the name. In contrast to all previous individualistic and near-anarchistic thinkers, such as La Boétie, Hodgskin or the young Fichte, Molinari did not base the brunt of his argument on a moral opposition to the State. While an ardent individualist, Molinari grounded his argument on free-market, *laissez-faire*

economics, and proceeded logically to ask
the question: If the free market can and
should supply *all other* goods and services,
why not also the services of protection?

During the same year, 1849, Molinari
expanded his radically new theory into
a book, *Les Soirées de la Rue Saint-Lazare*,
a series of fictional dialogues between
three people: the Conservative (advo-
cate of high tariffs and state monopoly
privileges), the Socialist, and the Economist (himself). The final dialogue elabo-
rated further on his theory of free-market protective services. Four decades
later, in his *Les Lois Naturelles de l'Economie
Politique* (1887), Molinari was still a firm
believer in privately competitive police
companies, public works companies, and
defense companies. Unfortunately, in his
only work to be translated into English,
La Societé Future (*The Society of Tomorrow*,
New York: G.P. Putnam's Sons, 1904),
Molinari had partially retreated to an
advocacy of a single monopoly private

defense and protection company, rather than allowing free competition.

It is instructive to note the storm of contention that Molinari's article and his *Soirées* brought about in the *laissez-faire* stalwarts of French economics. A meeting of the Societe d'Economie Politique in 1849 was devoted to Molinari's daring new book, the *Soirées*. Charles Coquelin opined that justice needs a "supreme authority," and that no competition in any area can exist without the supreme authority of the State. In a similarly unsupported and *a priori* fulmination, Frédéric Bastiat declared that justice and security can only be guaranteed by force, *and* that force can *only* be the attribute of a "supreme power," the State. Neither commentator bothered to engage in a critique of Molinari's arguments.

Only Charles Dunoyer did so, complaining that Molinari had been carried away by the "illusions of logic," and maintaining that "competition between governmental companies is chimerical, because it leads to violent battles." Dunoyer, instead, chose to rely on the "competition" of political parties within representative government—hardly a satisfactory libertarian solution to the problem of social conflict! He also opined that it was most prudent to leave force in the hands of the State, "where civilization has put it"—this is from one of the great founders of the conquest theory of the State!

Unfortunately, this critical issue was barely treated in the meeting, since the discussion largely centered on Dunoyer's and the other economists' criticizing Molinari for going too far in attacking all uses of eminent domain by the State. (See *Journal des Economistes* XXIV (October 15, 1849: 315–16.)

With this publication of Professor McCulloch's translation of Molinari's original article, let us hope that Molinari will now come to the attention of scholars and translators.

The Production
of Security[1]

Gustave de Molinari

There are two ways of consider-
ing society. According to some,
the development of human asso-
ciations is not subject to providential,
unchangeable laws. Rather, these associ-
ations, having originally been organized
in a purely artificial manner by primeval

---

[1] Although this article may appear utopian in its conclusions,
we nevertheless believe that we should publish it in order to
attract the attention of economists and journalists to a question which has hitherto been treated in only a desultory manner and which should, nevertheless, in our day and age, be
approached with greater precision. So many people exag-
gerate the nature and prerogatives of government that it has
become useful to formulate strictly the boundaries outside of
which the intervention of authority becomes anarchical and
tyrannical rather than protective and profitable. [Note of the
editor-in-chief of the *Journal des Economistes*, 1849.]

legislators, can later be modified or remade by other legislators, in step with the progress of *social science*. In this system the government plays a preeminent role, because it is upon it, the custodian of the principle of authority, that the daily task of modifying and remaking society devolves.

According to others, on the contrary, society is a purely natural fact. Like the earth on which it stands, society moves in accordance with general, preexisting laws. In this system, there is no such thing, strictly speaking, as social science; there is only economic science, which studies the natural organism of society and shows how this organism functions.

We propose to examine, within the latter system, the function and natural organization of government.

The Natural Order
of Society

In order to define and delimit the function of government, it is first necessary to investigate the essence and object of society itself. What natural impulse do men obey when they combine into society? They are obeying the impulse, or, to speak more exactly, the instinct of sociability. The human race is essentially *sociable*. Like beavers and the higher animal species in general, men have an instinctive inclination to live in society.

Why did this instinct come into being?

Man experiences a multitude of needs, on whose satisfaction his happiness depends, and whose non-satisfaction entails suffering. Alone and isolated, he could only provide in an incomplete, insufficient manner for these incessant needs. The instinct of sociability brings him together with similar persons, and drives him into communication with them. Therefore, impelled by the *self-interest* of the individuals thus brought together, a certain *division of labor* is established, necessarily followed by *exchanges*. In brief, we see an *organization* emerge, by means of which man can more completely satisfy his needs than he could living in isolation.

This natural organization is called *society*.

The object of society is therefore the most complete satisfaction of man's needs. The division of labor and exchange are the means by which this is accomplished.

Among the needs of man, there is one particular type which plays an immense role in the history of humanity, namely the need for security.

What is this need?

It is in one's self-interest to procure security at the lowest price possible.

Whether they live in isolation or in society, men are, above all, interested in preserving their existence and the fruits of their labor. If the sense of justice were universally prevalent on earth; if, consequently, each man confined himself to laboring and exchanging the fruits of his labor, without wishing to take away, by violence or fraud, the fruits of other men's labor; if everyone had, in one word, an instinctive horror of any act harmful to another person, it is certain that security would exist *naturally* on earth, and that no artificial institution would be necessary to establish it. Unfortunately this is not the way things are. The sense of justice seems to be the perquisite of only a few eminent and exceptional temperaments. Among the inferior races, it exists only in a rudimentary state. Hence the innumerable criminal attempts, ever since the beginning of the world, since the days of Cain and Abel, against the lives and property of individuals.

Hence also the creation of establishments whose object is to guarantee to everyone the peaceful possession of his person and his goods.

These establishments were called *governments*.

Everywhere, even among the least enlightened tribes, one encounters a government, so universal and urgent is the need for security provided by government.

Everywhere, men resign themselves to the most extreme sacrifices rather than do without government and hence security, without realizing that in so doing, they misjudge their alternatives.

Suppose that a man found his person and his means of survival incessantly menaced; wouldn't his first and constant preoccupation be to protect himself from the dangers that surround him? This preoccupation, these efforts, this labor, would necessarily absorb the greater portion of his time, as well as the most energetic and active faculties of his intelligence. In consequence, he could only devote insufficient and uncertain efforts, and his divided attention, to the satisfaction of his other needs.

Even though this man might be asked to surrender a very considerable portion of his time and of his labor to someone who takes it upon himself to guarantee the peaceful possession of his person and his goods, wouldn't it be to his advantage to conclude this bargain?

Still, it would obviously be no less in his self-interest to procure his *security* at the lowest price possible.

Competition in Security

If there is one well-established truth in political economy, it is this:

That in all cases, for all commodities that serve to provide for the tangible or intangible needs of the consumer, it is in the consumer's best interest that labor and trade remain free, because the freedom of labor and of trade have as their necessary and permanent result the maximum reduction of price.

And this:

That the interests of the consumer of any commodity whatsoever should always prevail over the interests of the producer.

Now in pursuing these principles, one arrives at this rigorous conclusion:

That the production of security should, in the interests of the consumers of this intangible commodity, remain subject to the law of free competition.

Whence it follows:

That no government should have the right to prevent another government from going into competition with it, or to require consumers of security to come exclusively to it for this commodity.

Nevertheless, I must admit that, up until the present, one recoiled before this rigorous implication of the principle of free competition.

One economist who has done as much as anyone to extend the application of the principle of liberty, Charles Dunoyer, thinks "that the functions of government will never be able to fall into the domain of private activity."[2]

Now here is a citation of a clear and obvious exception to the principle of free competition.

---

[2] In his remarkable book *De la liberté du travail* (On the Freedom of Labor), Vol. III, p. 253. (Published by Guillaumin.)

This exception is all the more remarkable for being unique.

Undoubtedly, one can find economists who establish more numerous exceptions to this principle; but we may emphatically affirm that these are not *pure* economists. True economists are generally agreed, on the one hand, that the government should restrict itself to guaranteeing the security of its citizens, and on the other hand, that the freedom of labor and of trade should otherwise be whole and absolute.

But why should there be an exception relative to security? What special reason is there that the production of security cannot be relegated to free competition? Why should it be subjected to a different principle and organized according to a different system?

On this point, the masters of the science are silent, and Dunoyer, who has clearly noted this exception, does not investigate the grounds on which it is based.

Security an Exception?

We are consequently led to ask ourselves whether his exception is well founded, in the eyes of the economist.

It offends reason to believe that a well-established natural law can admit of exceptions. A natural law must hold everywhere and always, or be invalid. I cannot believe, for example, that the universal law of gravitation, which governs the physical world, is ever suspended in any instance or at any point of the universe. Now I consider economic laws comparable to natural laws, and I have just as much faith in the principle of the division of labor as I have in the universal law of gravitation. I believe that while these principles can be *disturbed*, they admit of no exceptions.

But, if this is the case, the production of security should not be removed from the jurisdiction of free competition; and if it is removed, society as a whole suffers a loss.

Either this is logical and true, or else the principles on which economic science is based are invalid.

The Alternatives

It thus has been demonstrated *a priori*, to those of us who have faith in the principles of economic science, that the exception indicated above is not justified, and that the production of security, like anything else, should be subject to the law of free competition.

Once we have acquired this conviction, what remains for us to do? It remains for us to investigate how it has come about that the production of security has not been subjected to the law of free competition, but rather has been subjected to different principles.

What are those principles?

Those of *monopoly* and *communism*.

In the entire world, there is not a single establishment of the security industry that is not based on monopoly or on communism.

In this connection, we add, in passing, a simple remark.

Political economy has disapproved equally of monopoly and communism in the various branches of human activity, wherever it has found them. Is it not then strange and unreasonable that it accepts them in the security industry?

Monopoly
and Communism

L et us now examine how it is that all known governments have either been subjected to the law of monopoly, or else organized according to the communistic principle.

First let us investigate what is understood by the words monopoly and communism.

It is an observable truth that the more urgent and necessary are man's needs, the greater will be the sacrifices he will be willing to endure in order to satisfy them. Now, there are some things that are found abundantly in nature, and whose production does not require a great expenditure of labor, but which, since they satisfy these urgent and necessary wants, can consequently acquire an exchange value all out of proportion with their natural value. Take salt for example. Suppose that a man or a group of men succeed in having the exclusive production and sale of salt assigned to themselves. It is apparent that this man or group could raise the price of this commodity well above its value, well above the price it would have under a regime of free competition.

One will then say that this man or this group possesses a monopoly, and that the price of salt is a monopoly price.

But it is obvious that the consumers will not consent freely to paying the abusive monopoly surtax. It will be necessary to compel them to pay it, and in order to compel them, the employment of force will be necessary.

Every monopoly necessarily rests on force.

When the monopolists are no longer as strong as the consumers they exploit, what happens?

In every instance, the monopoly finally disappears either violently or as the outcome of an amicable transaction. What is it replaced with?

If the roused and insurgent consumers secure the means of production of the salt industry, in all probability they will confiscate this industry for their own profit, and their first thought will be, not to relegate it to free competition, but rather to exploit it, *in common*, for their own account. They will then name a director or a directive committee to operate the saltworks, to whom they will allocate the funds necessary to defray the costs of salt production. Then, since the experience of the past will have made them suspicious and distrustful, since they will be afraid that the director named by them will seize production for his own benefit, and simply reconstitute by open or hidden means the old monopoly for his own profit, they will elect delegates, representatives entrusted with appropriating the funds necessary for production, with watching over their use, and with making sure that the salt produced is equally distributed to those entitled to it. The production of salt will be organized in this manner.

This form of the organization of production has been named communism.

When this organization is applied to a single commodity, the communism is said to be partial.

When it is applied to all commodities, the communism is said to be complete.

But whether communism is partial or complete, political economy is no more tolerant of it than it is of monopoly, of which it is merely an extension.

The Monopolization and Collectivization of the Security Industry

Isn't what has just been said about salt applicable to security? Isn't this the history of all monarchies and all republics?

Everywhere, the production of security began by being organized as a monopoly, and everywhere, nowadays, it tends to be organized communistically.

Here is why.

Among the tangible and intangible commodities necessary to man, none, with the possible exception of wheat, is more indispensable, and therefore none can support quite so large a monopoly duty.

Nor is any quite so prone to monopolization.

What, indeed, is the situation of men who need security? Weakness. What is the situation of those who undertake to provide them with this necessary security? Strength. If it were otherwise, if the consumers of security were stronger than the producers, they obviously would dispense with their assistance.

Now, if the producers of security are originally stronger than the consumers, won't it be easy for the former to impose a monopoly on the latter?

Everywhere, when societies originate, we see the strongest, most warlike races seizing the exclusive government of the society. Everywhere we see these races seizing a monopoly on security within certain more or less extensive boundaries, depending on their number and strength.

And, this monopoly being, by its very nature, extraordinarily profitable, everywhere we see the races invested with the monopoly on security devoting themselves to bitter struggles, in order to add to *the extent of their market*, the number of their *forced* consumers, and hence the amount of their gains.

War has been the necessary and inevitable consequence of the establishment of a monopoly on security.

Another inevitable consequence has been that this monopoly has engendered all other monopolies.

When they saw the situation of the monopolizers of security, the producers of other commodities could not help but notice that nothing in the world is more advantageous than monopoly. They, in turn, were consequently tempted to add to the gains from their own industry by the same process. But what did they require in order to monopolize, to the detriment of the consumers, the commodity they produced? They required force. However, they did not possess the force necessary to constrain the consumers in question. What did they do? They borrowed it, for a consideration, from those who had it. They petitioned and obtained, at the price of an agreed upon fee, the exclusive privilege of carrying on their industry within certain determined boundaries. Since the fees for these privileges brought the producers of security a goodly sum of money, the world was soon covered with monopolies. Labor and trade were everywhere shackled, enchained, and the condition of the masses remained as miserable as possible.

Nevertheless, after long centuries of suffering, as enlightenment spread through the world little by little, the masses who had been smothered under this nexus of privileges began to rebel against the privileged, and to demand *liberty*, that is to say, the suppression of monopolies.

This process took many forms. What happened in England, for example? Originally, the race which governed the country and which was militarily organized (the aristocracy), having at its head a hereditary leader (the king), and an equally hereditary administrative council (the House of Lords), set the price of security, which it had monopolized, at whatever rate it pleased. There was no negotiation between the producers of security and the consumers. This was the rule of *absolutism*. But as time passed, the consumers, having become aware of their numbers and strength, arose against the purely arbitrary regime, and they obtained the right to negotiate with the producers over the price of the commodity. For this purpose, they sent delegates to the *House of Commons* to discuss the level of taxes, the price of security. They were thus able to improve their lot somewhat. Nevertheless, the producers of security had a direct say in the naming of the members of the House of Commons, so that debate was not entirely open, and the price of the commodity remained above its natural value.

One day the exploited consumers rose against the producers and dispossessed them of their industry. They then undertook to carry on this industry by themselves and chose for this purpose a director of operations assisted by a Council. Thus communism replaced monopoly. But the scheme did not work, and twenty years later, primitive monopoly was reestablished. Only this time the monopolists were wise enough not to restore the rule of absolutism; they accepted free debate over taxes, being careful, all the while, incessantly to corrupt the delegates of the opposition party. They gave these delegates control over various posts in the administration of security, and they even went so far as to allow the most influential into the bosom of their superior Council. Nothing could have been more clever than this behavior. Nevertheless, the consumers of security finally became aware of these abuses, and demanded the reform of Parliament. This long-contested reform was finally achieved, and since that time, the consumers have won a significant lightening of their burdens.

In France, the monopoly on security, after having similarly undergone frequent vicissitudes and various modifications, has just been overthrown for the second time.[3] As once happened in England, monopoly for the benefit of one caste, and then in the name of a certain class of society, was finally replaced by communal production. The consumers as a whole, behaving like shareholders, named a director responsible for supervising the actions of the director and of his administration.

We will content ourselves with making one simple observation on the subject of this new regime.

Just as the monopoly on security logically had to spawn universal monopoly,

---

[3] Translator's note: De Molinari was writing one year after the revolutions of 1848.

so communistic security must logically spawn universal communism.

In reality, we have a choice of two things:

Either communistic production is superior to free production, or it is not.

If it is, then it must be for all things, not just for security.

If not, *progress* requires that it be replaced by free production.

Complete communism or complete liberty: that is the alternative!

Government and Society

But is it conceivable that the production of security could be organized other than as a monopoly or communistically? Could it conceivably be relegated to free competition?

The response to this question on the part of *political* writers is unanimous: No.

Why? We will tell you why.

Because these writers, who are concerned especially with governments, know nothing about society. They regard it as an artificial fabrication, and believe that the mission of government is to modify and remake it constantly.

Now in order to modify or remake society, it is necessary to be empowered with an *authority* superior to that of the various individuals of which it is composed.

Monopolistic governments claim to have obtained from God himself this authority which gives them the right to modify or remake society according to their fancy, and to dispose of persons and property however they please. Communistic governments appeal to human reason, as manifested in the majority of the sovereign people.

But do monopolistic governments and communistic governments truly possess this superior, irresistible authority? Do they in reality have a higher authority than that which a free government could have? This is what we must investigate.

The Divine Right
of Kings and Majorities

If it were true that society were not *naturally* organized, if it were true that the laws which govern its motion were to be constantly modified or remade, the *legislators* would necessarily have to have an immutable, sacred authority. Being the continuators of Providence on earth, they would have to be regarded as almost equal to God. If it were otherwise, would it not be impossible for them to fulfill their mission? Indeed, one cannot intervene in human affairs, one cannot attempt to direct and regulate them, without daily offending a multitude of interests. Unless those in power are believed to have a mandate from a superior entity, the injured interests will resist.

Whence the fiction of divine right.

43

This fiction was certainly the best imaginable. If you succeed in persuading the multitude that God himself has chosen certain men or certain races to give laws to society and to govern it, no one will dream of revolting against these appointees of Providence, and everything the government does will be accepted. A government based on divine right is imperishable.

On one condition only, namely that divine right is believed in.

If one takes the thought into one's head that the leaders of the people do not receive their inspirations directly from providence itself, that they obey purely human impulses, the prestige that surrounds them will disappear. One will irreverently resist their sovereign decisions, as one resists anything man-made whose *utility* has not been clearly demonstrated.

It is accordingly fascinating to see the pains theoreticians of the divine right take to establish the *superhumanity* of the races in possession of human government.

Let us listen, for example, to Joseph de Maistre:

> Man does not make sovereigns. At the very most he can serve as an instrument for dispossessing one sovereign and handing his State over to another sovereign, himself already a prince. Moreover, there has never existed a sovereign family traceable to plebeian origins. If this phenomenon were to appear, it would mark a new epoch on earth.
>
> ... It is written: *I am the Maker of sovereigns*. This is not just a religious slogan, a preacher's metaphor; it is the literal truth pure and simple. It is a law of the political world. God *makes* kings, word for word. He prepares royal races, nurtures them at the center of a cloud which hides their origins. Finally they

appear, *crowned with glory and honor,* they take their places.[4]

According to this system, which embodies the will of Providence in certain men and which invests these chosen ones, these anointed ones with a quasi-divine authority, the *subjects* evidently have no rights at all. They must submit, *without question,* to the decrees of the sovereign authority, as if they were the decrees of Providence itself.

According to Plutarch, the body is the instrument of the soul, and the soul is the instrument of God. According to the divine right school, God selects certain souls and uses them as instruments for governing the world.

If men *had faith* in this theory, surely nothing could unsettle a government based on divine right.

[4] *Du principe générateur des constitutions politiques* (On the Generating Principle of Political Constitutions) Preface.

Unfortunately, they have completely lost faith.

Why?

Because one fine day they took it into their heads to question and to reason, and in questioning, in reasoning, they discovered that their governors governed them no better than they, simply mortals out of communication with Providence, could have done themselves.

It was *free inquiry* that demonetized the fiction of divine right, to the point where the subjects of monarchs or of aristocracies based on divine right obey them only insofar as they think it *in their own self-interest* to obey them.

Has the communist fiction fared any better?

According to the communist theory, of which Rousseau is the high-priest, authority does not descend from on high, but rather comes up from below. The government no longer looks to Providence for its authority, it looks to united mankind, to the *one, indivisible, and sovereign* nation.

Here is what the communists, the partisans of popular sovereignty, assume. They assume that human reason has the power to discover the best laws and the organization which most perfectly suits society; and that, in practice, these laws reveal themselves at the conclusion of a free debate between conflicting opinions. If there is no unanimity, if there is still dissension after the debate, the majority is in the right, since it comprises the larger number of reasonable individuals. (These individuals are, of course, assumed to be equal, otherwise the whole structure collapses.) Consequently, they insist that the decisions of the majority must become *law*, and that the minority is obliged to submit to it, even if it is contrary to its most deeply rooted convictions and injures its most precious interests.

That is the theory; but, in practice, does the *authority* of the decision of the majority really have this irresistible, absolute character as assumed? Is it always, in every instance, respected by the minority? Could it be?

Let us take an example.

Let us suppose that socialism succeeds in propagating itself among the working classes in the countryside as it has already among the working classes in the cities; that it consequently becomes the majority in the country and that, profiting from this situation, it sends a socialist majority to the Legislative Assembly and names a socialist president. Suppose that this majority and this president, invested with sovereign authority, decrees the imposition of a tax on the rich of three billion, in order to organize the labor of the poor, as Proudhon demanded. Is it probable that the minority would submit peacefully to his iniquitous and absurd, yet legal, yet *constitutional* plunder?

No, without a doubt it would not hesitate to disown *the authority* of the majority and to defend its property.

Under this regime, as under the preceding, one obeys the custodians of authority only insofar as one thinks it in one's self-interest to obey them.

This leads us to affirm that the moral foundation of authority is neither as solid nor as wide, under a regime of monopoly or of communism, as it could be under a regime of liberty.

The Regime of Terror

Suppose nevertheless that the partisans of an *artificial organization*, either the monopolists or the communists, are right; that society is not naturally organized, and that the task of making and unmaking the laws that regulate society continuously devolves upon men, look in what a lamentable situation the world would find itself. The moral authority of governors rests, *in reality*, on the self-interest of the governed. The latter having a natural tendency to resist anything harmful to their self-interest, unacknowledged authority would continually require the help of physical force.

The monopolist and the communists, furthermore, completely understand this necessity.

If anyone, says M. de Maistre, attempts to detract from the authority of God's chosen ones, let him be turned over to the secular power, let the hangman perform his office.

If anyone does not recognize the authority of those chosen by the people, say the theoreticians of the school of Rousseau, if he resists any decision whatsoever of the majority, let him be punished as an enemy of the sovereign people, let the guillotine perform justice.

These two schools, which both take *artificial organization* as their point of departure, necessarily lead to the same conclusion: TERROR.

The Free Market
for Security

Allow us now to formulate a simple hypothetical situation.

Let us imagine a new-born society: The men who compose it are busy working and exchanging the fruits of their labor. A natural instinct reveals to these men that their persons, the land they occupy and cultivate, the fruits of their labor, are their *property*, and that no one, except themselves, has the right to dispose of or touch this property. This instinct is not hypothetical; it exists. But man being an imperfect creature, this awareness of the right of everyone to his person and his goods will not be found to the same degree in every soul, and certain individuals will make criminal attempts, by violence or by fraud, against the persons or the property of others.

Hence, the need for an industry that prevents or suppresses these forcible or fraudulent aggressions.

Let us suppose that a man or a combination of men comes and says:

For a recompense, I will undertake to prevent or suppress criminal attempts against persons and property.

Let those who wish their persons and property to be sheltered from all aggression apply to me.

Before striking a bargain with this *producer of security*, what will the consumers do?

In the first place, they will check if he is really strong enough to protect them.

In the second place, whether his character is such that they will not have to worry about his instigating the very aggressions he is supposed to suppress.

In the third place, whether any other producer of security, offering equal guarantees, is disposed to offer them this commodity on better terms.

These terms are of various kinds.

In order to be able to guarantee the consumers full security of their persons and property, and, in case of harm, to give them a compensation proportioned to the loss suffered, it would be necessary, indeed:

1. That the producer establish certain penalties against the offenders of persons and the violators of property, and that the consumers agree to submit to these penalties, in case they themselves commit offenses;

2. That he impose certain inconveniences on the consumers, with the object of facilitating the discovery of the authors of offenses;

3. That he regularly gather, in order to cover his costs of production as well as an appropriate return

for his efforts, a certain sum, variable according to the situation of the consumers, the particular occupations they engage in, and the extent, value, and nature of their properties.

If these terms, necessary for carrying on this industry, are agreeable to the consumers, a bargain will be struck. Otherwise the consumers will either do without security, or else apply to another producer.

Now if we consider the particular nature of the security industry, it is apparent that the producers will necessarily restrict their clientele to certain territorial boundaries. They would be unable to cover their costs if they tried to provide police services in localities comprising only a few clients. Their clientele will naturally be clustered around the center of their activities. They would nevertheless be unable to abuse this situation by dictating to the consumers. In the event of an abusive rise in the price of security,

the consumers would always have the
option of giving their patronage to a
new entrepreneur, or to a neighboring
entrepreneur.

This option the consumer[5] retains of
being able to buy security wherever he

---

[5] Adam Smith, whose remarkable spirit of observation
extends to all subjects, remarks that the administration of justice gained much, in England, from the competition between
the different courts of law:

> The fees of court seem originally to have been
> the principal support of the different courts of jus-
> tice in England. Each court endeavoured to draw to
> itself as much business as it could, and was, upon that
> account, willing to take cognizance of many suits
> which were not originally intended to fall under its
> jurisdiction. The court of king's bench instituted for
> the trial of criminal causes only, took cognizance of
> civil suits; the plaintiff pretending that the defendant,
> in not doing him justice, had been guilty of some
> trespass or misdemeanor. The court of exchequer,
> instituted for the levying of the king's revenue, and
> for enforcing the payment of such debts only as were
> due to the king, took cognizance of all other contract
> debts; the plaintiff alleging that he could not pay the
> king, because the defendant would not pay him. In
> consequence of such fictions it came, in many case,
> to depend altogether upon the parties before what
> court they would chuse to have their cause tried;
> and each court endeavoured, by superior dispatch
> and impartiality, to draw to itself as many causes as

pleases brings about a constant emulation among all the producers, each producer striving to maintain or augment his clientele with the attraction of cheapness or of faster, more complete and better justice.

If, on the contrary, the consumer is not free to buy security wherever he pleases, you forthwith see open up a large profession dedicated to arbitrariness and bad management. justice becomes slow and costly, the police vexatious, individual liberty is no longer respected, the price of security is abusively inflated and inequitably apportioned, according to the power and influence of this or that class of consumers. The protectors engage in bitter struggles to wrest customers from one

---

it could. The present admirable constitution of the courts of justice in England was, perhaps, originally in a great measure, formed by this emulation, which anciently took place between their respective judges; each judge endeavouring to give, in his own court, the speediest and most effectual remedy, which the law would admit, for every sort of injustice. (*The Wealth of Nations* [New York: Modern Library, 1937]; originally 1776), p. 679)

another. In a word, all the abuses inherent in monopoly or in communism crop up.

Under the rule of free competition, war between the producers of security entirely loses its justification. Why would they make war? To conquer consumers? But the consumers would not allow themselves to be conquered. They would be careful not to allow themselves to be protected by men who would unscrupulously attack the persons and property of their rivals. If some audacious conqueror tried to become dictator, they would immediately call to their aid all the free consumers menaced by this aggression, and they would treat him as he deserved. Just as war is the natural consequence of monopoly, peace is the natural consequence of liberty.

Under a regime of liberty, the natural organization of the security industry would not be different from that of other industries. In small districts a single entrepreneur could suffice. This entrepreneur might leave his business to his son, or sell it to another entrepreneur. In larger districts, one company by itself would bring together enough resources adequately to carry on this important and difficult business. If it were well managed, this company could easily last, and security would last with it. In the security industry, just as in most of the other branches of production, the latter mode of organization will probably replace the former, in the end.

On the one hand this would be a monarchy, and on the other hand it would be a republic; but it would be a monarchy without monopoly and a republic without communism.

On either hand, this authority would be accepted and respected in the name of *utility*, and would not be an authority imposed by *terror*.

It will undoubtedly be disputed whether such a hypothetical situation is realizable. But, at the risk of being considered utopian, we affirm that this is not disputable, that a careful examination of the facts will decide the problem of government more and more in favor of liberty, just as it does all other economic problems. We are convinced, so far as we are concerned, that one day societies will be established to agitate for the *freedom of government*, as they have already been established on behalf of the freedom of commerce.

And we do not hesitate to add that after this reform has been achieved, and all artificial obstacles to the free action of the natural laws that govern the economic world have disappeared, the situation of the various members of society will become *the best possible*.

NOTE

Gustave de Molinari (March 3, 1819–January 28, 1912) was a Belgian-born economist associated with the French "économistes," a group of laissez-faire liberals. Throughout his life, Molinari defended peace, free trade, freedom of speech, freedom of association, and liberty in all its forms. He was the originator of the theory of Market Anarchism.

Printed in Great Britain
by Amazon

54604854R00037